MOVIE RE

—— LOG BOOK ——

Are you enjoying this awesome Log Book?

If so, please leave us a review. We are very interested in your feedback
to create even better products for you to enjoy shortly.

Shopping for Log Books can be fun.
Visit our website at amazing-notebooks.com or scan the QR
code below to see all of our awesome and creative products!

Thank you very much!

Amazing Notebooks

www.amazing-notebooks.com

MOVIE REVIEWS
— LOG BOOK —

INFORMATION

NAME

ADDRESS

E-MAIL ADDRESS

WEBSITE

PHONE   FAX

EMERGENCY CONTACT PERSON

PHONE   FAX

Movie Review Log Book

TITLE:

GENRE: **YEAR:**

LENGTH: **DIRECTOR:**

DATE SEEN: **WHERE?**

COMPANY: **RATING (G, PG, G13, R):**

AWARDS:

ACTORS

....
....
....
....
....

MOVIE REVIEW (Storyline / Plot / Memorable Quotes)

....
....
....
....
....
....
....
....
....
....
....
....

RATINGS

CAST: **DRIECTOR:**

SCREENPLAY: **EFFECTS:**

COSTUMES: **MUSIC:**

PRODUCTION DESIGN: **CINEMATOGRAPHY:**

Overall Rating ★ ★ ★ ★ ★   *Watch Again?* **Y:** **/ N:**

Movie Review Log Book

TITLE:

GENRE: **YEAR:**

LENGTH: **DIRECTOR:**

DATE SEEN: **WHERE?**

COMPANY: **RATING (G, PG, G13, R):**

AWARDS:

ACTORS

MOVIE REVIEW (Storyline / Plot / Memorable Quotes)

RATINGS

CAST: **DRIECTOR:**

SCREENPLAY: **EFFECTS:**

COSTUMES: **MUSIC:**

PRODUCTION DESIGN: **CINEMATOGRAPHY:**

Overall Rating ★ ★ ★ ★ ★   *Watch Again?* Y: / N:

Movie Review Log Book

TITLE:

GENRE: **YEAR:**

LENGTH: **DIRECTOR:**

DATE SEEN: **WHERE?**

COMPANY: **RATING (G, PG, G13, R):**

AWARDS:

ACTORS

....
....
....
....
....

MOVIE REVIEW (Storyline / Plot / Memorable Quotes)

....
....
....
....
....
....
....
....
....
....
....
....

RATINGS

CAST: **DRIECTOR:**

SCREENPLAY: **EFFECTS:**

COSTUMES: **MUSIC:**

PRODUCTION DESIGN: **CINEMATOGRAPHY:**

Overall Rating ★ ★ ★ ★ ★ *Watch Again?* **Y:** **/ N:**

Movie Review Log Book

TITLE:

GENRE: **YEAR:**

LENGTH: **DIRECTOR:**

DATE SEEN: **WHERE?**

COMPANY: **RATING (G, PG, G13, R):**

AWARDS:

ACTORS

MOVIE REVIEW (Storyline / Plot / Memorable Quotes)

RATINGS

CAST: **DRIECTOR:**

SCREENPLAY: **EFFECTS:**

COSTUMES: **MUSIC:**

PRODUCTION DESIGN: **CINEMATOGRAPHY:**

Overall Rating ★ ★ ★ ★ ★   *Watch Again?* **Y:**   **/ N:**

Movie Review Log Book

TITLE:

GENRE: **YEAR:**

LENGTH: **DIRECTOR:**

DATE SEEN: **WHERE?**

COMPANY: **RATING (G, PG, G13, R):**

AWARDS:

ACTORS

....
....
....
....
....

MOVIE REVIEW (Storyline / Plot / Memorable Quotes)

....
....
....
....
....
....
....
....
....
....
....
....

RATINGS

CAST: **DRIECTOR:**

SCREENPLAY: **EFFECTS:**

COSTUMES: **MUSIC:**

PRODUCTION DESIGN: **CINEMATOGRAPHY:**

Overall Rating ★ ★ ★ ★ ★   *Watch Again?* **Y:** / **N:**

Movie Review Log Book

TITLE:

GENRE: **YEAR:**

LENGTH: **DIRECTOR:**

DATE SEEN: **WHERE?**

COMPANY: **RATING (G, PG, G13, R):**

AWARDS:

ACTORS

MOVIE REVIEW (Storyline / Plot / Memorable Quotes)

RATINGS

CAST: **DRIECTOR:**

SCREENPLAY: **EFFECTS:**

COSTUMES: **MUSIC:**

PRODUCTION DESIGN: **CINEMATOGRAPHY:**

Overall Rating ★ ★ ★ ★ ★ *Watch Again?* Y: / N:

Movie Review Log Book

TITLE:

GENRE: **YEAR:**

LENGTH: **DIRECTOR:**

DATE SEEN: **WHERE?**

COMPANY: **RATING (G, PG, G13, R):**

AWARDS:

ACTORS

MOVIE REVIEW (Storyline / Plot / Memorable Quotes)

RATINGS

CAST: **DRIECTOR:**

SCREENPLAY: **EFFECTS:**

COSTUMES: **MUSIC:**

PRODUCTION DESIGN: **CINEMATOGRAPHY:**

Overall Rating ★ ★ ★ ★ ★   *Watch Again?* **Y:**   **/ N:**

Movie Review Log Book

TITLE:

GENRE: **YEAR:**

LENGTH: **DIRECTOR:**

DATE SEEN: **WHERE?**

COMPANY: **RATING (G, PG, G13, R):**

AWARDS:

ACTORS

....
....
....
....
....

MOVIE REVIEW (Storyline / Plot / Memorable Quotes)

....
....
....
....
....
....
....
....
....
....
....
....

RATINGS

CAST: **DRIECTOR:**

SCREENPLAY: **EFFECTS:**

COSTUMES: **MUSIC:**

PRODUCTION DESIGN: **CINEMATOGRAPHY:**

Overall Rating ★ ★ ★ ★ ★   *Watch Again?* **Y:**   **/ N:**

Movie Review Log Book

TITLE:

GENRE: **YEAR:**

LENGTH: **DIRECTOR:**

DATE SEEN: **WHERE?**

COMPANY: **RATING (G, PG, G13, R):**

AWARDS:

ACTORS

MOVIE REVIEW (Storyline / Plot / Memorable Quotes)

RATINGS

CAST: **DRIECTOR:**

SCREENPLAY: **EFFECTS:**

COSTUMES: **MUSIC:**

PRODUCTION DESIGN: **CINEMATOGRAPHY:**

Overall Rating ★ ★ ★ ★ ★   *Watch Again?* **Y:** **/ N:**

Movie Review Log Book

TITLE:

GENRE: **YEAR:**

LENGTH: **DIRECTOR:**

DATE SEEN: **WHERE?**

COMPANY: **RATING (G, PG, G13, R):**

AWARDS:

ACTORS

....
....
....
....
....

MOVIE REVIEW (Storyline / Plot / Memorable Quotes)

....
....
....
....
....
....
....
....
....
....
....
....

RATINGS

CAST: **DRIECTOR:**

SCREENPLAY: **EFFECTS:**

COSTUMES: **MUSIC:**

PRODUCTION DESIGN: **CINEMATOGRAPHY:**

Overall Rating ★ ★ ★ ★ ★   *Watch Again?* **Y:** **/ N:**

Movie Review Log Book

TITLE:

GENRE: **YEAR:**

LENGTH: **DIRECTOR:**

DATE SEEN: **WHERE?**

COMPANY: **RATING (G, PG, G13, R):**

AWARDS:

ACTORS

MOVIE REVIEW (Storyline / Plot / Memorable Quotes)

RATINGS

CAST: **DRIECTOR:**

SCREENPLAY: **EFFECTS:**

COSTUMES: **MUSIC:**

PRODUCTION DESIGN: **CINEMATOGRAPHY:**

Overall Rating ★ ★ ★ ★ ★ *Watch Again?* **Y:** **/ N:**

Movie Review Log Book

TITLE:

GENRE: **YEAR:**

LENGTH: **DIRECTOR:**

DATE SEEN: **WHERE?**

COMPANY: **RATING (G, PG, G13, R):**

AWARDS:

ACTORS

MOVIE REVIEW (Storyline / Plot / Memorable Quotes)

RATINGS

CAST: **DRIECTOR:**

SCREENPLAY: **EFFECTS:**

COSTUMES: **MUSIC:**

PRODUCTION DESIGN: **CINEMATOGRAPHY:**

Overall Rating ★ ★ ★ ★ ★   *Watch Again?* **Y:**   **/ N:**

Movie Review Log Book

TITLE:

GENRE: **YEAR:**

LENGTH: **DIRECTOR:**

DATE SEEN: **WHERE?**

COMPANY: **RATING (G, PG, G13, R):**

AWARDS:

ACTORS

....
....
....
....
....

MOVIE REVIEW (Storyline / Plot / Memorable Quotes)

....
....
....
....
....
....
....
....
....
....
....
....

RATINGS

CAST: **DRIECTOR:**

SCREENPLAY: **EFFECTS:**

COSTUMES: **MUSIC:**

PRODUCTION DESIGN: **CINEMATOGRAPHY:**

Overall Rating ★ ★ ★ ★ ★   *Watch Again?* **Y:** **/ N:**

Movie Review Log Book

TITLE:

GENRE: **YEAR:**

LENGTH: **DIRECTOR:**

DATE SEEN: **WHERE?**

COMPANY: **RATING (G, PG, G13, R):**

AWARDS:

ACTORS

MOVIE REVIEW (Storyline / Plot / Memorable Quotes)

RATINGS

CAST: **DRIECTOR:**

SCREENPLAY: **EFFECTS:**

COSTUMES: **MUSIC:**

PRODUCTION DESIGN: **CINEMATOGRAPHY:**

Overall Rating ⭐ ⭐ ⭐ ⭐ ⭐   *Watch Again?* **Y:** **/ N:**

Movie Review Log Book

TITLE:

GENRE: **YEAR:**

LENGTH: **DIRECTOR:**

DATE SEEN: **WHERE?**

COMPANY: **RATING (G, PG, G13, R):**

AWARDS:

ACTORS

....
....
....
....
....

MOVIE REVIEW (Storyline / Plot / Memorable Quotes)

....
....
....
....
....
....
....
....
....
....
....
....

RATINGS

CAST: **DRIECTOR:**

SCREENPLAY: **EFFECTS:**

COSTUMES: **MUSIC:**

PRODUCTION DESIGN: **CINEMATOGRAPHY:**

Overall Rating ★ ★ ★ ★ ★   *Watch Again?* **Y:** / **N:**

Movie Review Log Book

TITLE:

GENRE: **YEAR:**

LENGTH: **DIRECTOR:**

DATE SEEN: **WHERE?**

COMPANY: **RATING (G, PG, G13, R):**

AWARDS:

ACTORS

....
....
....
....
....

MOVIE REVIEW (Storyline / Plot / Memorable Quotes)

....
....
....
....
....
....
....
....
....
....
....
....

RATINGS

CAST: **DRIECTOR:**

SCREENPLAY: **EFFECTS:**

COSTUMES: **MUSIC:**

PRODUCTION DESIGN: **CINEMATOGRAPHY:**

Overall Rating ★ ★ ★ ★ ★   *Watch Again?* **Y:**   **/ N:**

Movie Review Log Book

TITLE:

GENRE: **YEAR:**

LENGTH: **DIRECTOR:**

DATE SEEN: **WHERE?**

COMPANY: **RATING (G, PG, G13, R):**

AWARDS:

ACTORS

....
....
....
....
....

MOVIE REVIEW (Storyline / Plot / Memorable Quotes)

....
....
....
....
....
....
....
....
....
....
....
....

RATINGS

CAST: **DRIECTOR:**

SCREENPLAY: **EFFECTS:**

COSTUMES: **MUSIC:**

PRODUCTION DESIGN: **CINEMATOGRAPHY:**

Overall Rating ★ ★ ★ ★ ★   *Watch Again?* **Y:** **/ N:**

Movie Review Log Book

TITLE:

GENRE: **YEAR:**

LENGTH: **DIRECTOR:**

DATE SEEN: **WHERE?**

COMPANY: **RATING (G, PG, G13, R):**

AWARDS:

ACTORS

....
....
....
....

MOVIE REVIEW (Storyline / Plot / Memorable Quotes)

....
....
....
....
....
....
....
....
....
....
....

RATINGS

CAST: **DRIECTOR:**

SCREENPLAY: **EFFECTS:**

COSTUMES: **MUSIC:**

PRODUCTION DESIGN: **CINEMATOGRAPHY:**

Overall Rating ★ ★ ★ ★ ★   *Watch Again?* **Y:** **/ N:**

Movie Review Log Book

TITLE:

GENRE: **YEAR:**

LENGTH: **DIRECTOR:**

DATE SEEN: **WHERE?**

COMPANY: **RATING (G, PG, G13, R):**

AWARDS:

ACTORS

....
....
....
....
....

MOVIE REVIEW (Storyline / Plot / Memorable Quotes)

....
....
....
....
....
....
....
....
....
....
....
....

RATINGS

CAST: **DRIECTOR:**

SCREENPLAY: **EFFECTS:**

COSTUMES: **MUSIC:**

PRODUCTION DESIGN: **CINEMATOGRAPHY:**

Overall Rating ★ ★ ★ ★ ★   *Watch Again?* **Y:** **/ N:**

Movie Review Log Book

TITLE:

GENRE: **YEAR:**

LENGTH: **DIRECTOR:**

DATE SEEN: **WHERE?**

COMPANY: **RATING (G, PG, G13, R):**

AWARDS:

ACTORS

....
....
....
....
....

MOVIE REVIEW (Storyline / Plot / Memorable Quotes)

....
....
....
....
....
....
....
....
....
....
....
....

RATINGS

CAST: **DRIECTOR:**

SCREENPLAY: **EFFECTS:**

COSTUMES: **MUSIC:**

PRODUCTION DESIGN: **CINEMATOGRAPHY:**

Overall Rating ★ ★ ★ ★ ★   *Watch Again?* **Y:**   **/ N:**

Movie Review Log Book

TITLE:

GENRE: **YEAR:**

LENGTH: **DIRECTOR:**

DATE SEEN: **WHERE?**

COMPANY: **RATING (G, PG, G13, R):**

AWARDS:

ACTORS

....
....
....
....
....

MOVIE REVIEW (Storyline / Plot / Memorable Quotes)

....
....
....
....
....
....
....
....
....
....
....
....

RATINGS

CAST: **DRIECTOR:**

SCREENPLAY: **EFFECTS:**

COSTUMES: **MUSIC:**

PRODUCTION DESIGN: **CINEMATOGRAPHY:**

Overall Rating ★ ★ ★ ★ ★ *Watch Again?* **Y:** **/ N:**

Movie Review Log Book

TITLE:

GENRE: **YEAR:**

LENGTH: **DIRECTOR:**

DATE SEEN: **WHERE?**

COMPANY: **RATING (G, PG, G13, R):**

AWARDS:

ACTORS

MOVIE REVIEW (Storyline / Plot / Memorable Quotes)

RATINGS

CAST: **DRIECTOR:**

SCREENPLAY: **EFFECTS:**

COSTUMES: **MUSIC:**

PRODUCTION DESIGN: **CINEMATOGRAPHY:**

Overall Rating ★ ★ ★ ★ ★   *Watch Again?* **Y: / N:**

Movie Review Log Book

TITLE:

GENRE: **YEAR:**

LENGTH: **DIRECTOR:**

DATE SEEN: **WHERE?**

COMPANY: **RATING (G, PG, G13, R):**

AWARDS:

ACTORS

....
....
....
....
....

MOVIE REVIEW (Storyline / Plot / Memorable Quotes)

....
....
....
....
....
....
....
....
....
....
....
....

RATINGS

CAST: **DRIECTOR:**

SCREENPLAY: **EFFECTS:**

COSTUMES: **MUSIC:**

PRODUCTION DESIGN: **CINEMATOGRAPHY:**

Overall Rating ★ ★ ★ ★ ★ *Watch Again?* **Y: / N:**

Movie Review Log Book

TITLE:

GENRE: **YEAR:**

LENGTH: **DIRECTOR:**

DATE SEEN: **WHERE?**

COMPANY: **RATING (G, PG, G13, R):**

AWARDS:

ACTORS

....
....
....
....
....

MOVIE REVIEW (Storyline / Plot / Memorable Quotes)

....
....
....
....
....
....
....
....
....
....

RATINGS

CAST: **DRIECTOR:**

SCREENPLAY: **EFFECTS:**

COSTUMES: **MUSIC:**

PRODUCTION DESIGN: **CINEMATOGRAPHY:**

Overall Rating ★ ★ ★ ★ ★   *Watch Again?* **Y:**   **/ N:**

Movie Review Log Book

TITLE:

GENRE: **YEAR:**

LENGTH: **DIRECTOR:**

DATE SEEN: **WHERE?**

COMPANY: **RATING (G, PG, G13, R):**

AWARDS:

ACTORS

....
....
....
....
....

MOVIE REVIEW (Storyline / Plot / Memorable Quotes)

....
....
....
....
....
....
....
....
....
....
....
....

RATINGS

CAST: **DRIECTOR:**

SCREENPLAY: **EFFECTS:**

COSTUMES: **MUSIC:**

PRODUCTION DESIGN: **CINEMATOGRAPHY:**

Overall Rating ★ ★ ★ ★ ★   *Watch Again?* **Y:** **/ N:**

Movie Review Log Book

TITLE:

GENRE: **YEAR:**

LENGTH: **DIRECTOR:**

DATE SEEN: **WHERE?**

COMPANY: **RATING (G, PG, G13, R):**

AWARDS:

ACTORS

MOVIE REVIEW (Storyline / Plot / Memorable Quotes)

RATINGS

CAST: **DRIECTOR:**

SCREENPLAY: **EFFECTS:**

COSTUMES: **MUSIC:**

PRODUCTION DESIGN: **CINEMATOGRAPHY:**

Overall Rating ☆ ☆ ☆ ☆ ☆ *Watch Again?* **Y:** **/ N:**

Movie Review Log Book

TITLE:

GENRE: **YEAR:**

LENGTH: **DIRECTOR:**

DATE SEEN: **WHERE?**

COMPANY: **RATING (G, PG, G13, R):**

AWARDS:

ACTORS

....
....
....
....
....

MOVIE REVIEW (Storyline / Plot / Memorable Quotes)

....
....
....
....
....
....
....
....
....
....
....
....
....

RATINGS

CAST: **DRIECTOR:**

SCREENPLAY: **EFFECTS:**

COSTUMES: **MUSIC:**

PRODUCTION DESIGN: **CINEMATOGRAPHY:**

Overall Rating ★ ★ ★ ★ ★   *Watch Again?* **Y:** **/ N:**

Movie Review Log Book

TITLE:

GENRE: **YEAR:**

LENGTH: **DIRECTOR:**

DATE SEEN: **WHERE?**

COMPANY: **RATING (G, PG, G13, R):**

AWARDS:

ACTORS

....
....
....
....

MOVIE REVIEW (Storyline / Plot / Memorable Quotes)

....
....
....
....
....
....
....
....
....
....
....

RATINGS

CAST: **DRIECTOR:**

SCREENPLAY: **EFFECTS:**

COSTUMES: **MUSIC:**

PRODUCTION DESIGN: **CINEMATOGRAPHY:**

Overall Rating ⭐ ⭐ ⭐ ⭐ ⭐   *Watch Again?* **Y:** **/ N:**

Movie Review Log Book

TITLE:

GENRE: **YEAR:**

LENGTH: **DIRECTOR:**

DATE SEEN: **WHERE?**

COMPANY: **RATING (G, PG, G13, R):**

AWARDS:

ACTORS

MOVIE REVIEW (Storyline / Plot / Memorable Quotes)

RATINGS

CAST: **DRIECTOR:**

SCREENPLAY: **EFFECTS:**

COSTUMES: **MUSIC:**

PRODUCTION DESIGN: **CINEMATOGRAPHY:**

Overall Rating ★ ★ ★ ★ ★   *Watch Again?* **Y:**   **/ N:**

Movie Review Log Book

TITLE:

GENRE: YEAR:

LENGTH: DIRECTOR:

DATE SEEN: WHERE?

COMPANY: RATING (G, PG, G13, R):

AWARDS:

ACTORS

....
....
....
....
....

MOVIE REVIEW (Storyline / Plot / Memorable Quotes)

....
....
....
....
....
....
....
....
....
....
....

RATINGS

CAST: DRIECTOR:

SCREENPLAY: EFFECTS:

COSTUMES: MUSIC:

PRODUCTION DESIGN: CINEMATOGRAPHY:

Overall Rating ★ ★ ★ ★ ★   Watch Again? Y: / N:

Movie Review Log Book

TITLE:

GENRE: YEAR:

LENGTH: DIRECTOR:

DATE SEEN: WHERE?

COMPANY: RATING (G, PG, G13, R):

AWARDS:

ACTORS

....
....
....
....
....

MOVIE REVIEW (Storyline / Plot / Memorable Quotes)

....
....
....
....
....
....
....
....
....
....
....

RATINGS

CAST: DRIECTOR:

SCREENPLAY: EFFECTS:

COSTUMES: MUSIC:

PRODUCTION DESIGN: CINEMATOGRAPHY:

Overall Rating ★ ★ ★ ★ ★   Watch Again? Y: / N:

Movie Review Log Book

TITLE:

GENRE: **YEAR:**

LENGTH: **DIRECTOR:**

DATE SEEN: **WHERE?**

COMPANY: **RATING (G, PG, G13, R):**

AWARDS:

ACTORS

....
....
....
....

MOVIE REVIEW (Storyline / Plot / Memorable Quotes)

....
....
....
....
....
....
....
....
....
....
....

RATINGS

CAST: **DRIECTOR:**

SCREENPLAY: **EFFECTS:**

COSTUMES: **MUSIC:**

PRODUCTION DESIGN: **CINEMATOGRAPHY:**

Overall Rating ★ ★ ★ ★ ★   *Watch Again?* **Y:** **/ N:**

Movie Review Log Book

TITLE:

GENRE: YEAR:

LENGTH: DIRECTOR:

DATE SEEN: WHERE?

COMPANY: RATING (G, PG, G13, R):

AWARDS:

ACTORS

MOVIE REVIEW (Storyline / Plot / Memorable Quotes)

RATINGS

CAST: DRIECTOR:

SCREENPLAY: EFFECTS:

COSTUMES: MUSIC:

PRODUCTION DESIGN: CINEMATOGRAPHY:

Overall Rating ⭐⭐⭐⭐⭐   Watch Again? Y: / N:

Movie Review Log Book

TITLE:

GENRE: **YEAR:**

LENGTH: **DIRECTOR:**

DATE SEEN: **WHERE?**

COMPANY: **RATING (G, PG, G13, R):**

AWARDS:

ACTORS

MOVIE REVIEW (Storyline / Plot / Memorable Quotes)

RATINGS

CAST: **DRIECTOR:**

SCREENPLAY: **EFFECTS:**

COSTUMES: **MUSIC:**

PRODUCTION DESIGN: **CINEMATOGRAPHY:**

Overall Rating ★ ★ ★ ★ ★   *Watch Again?* **Y:**   **/ N:**

Movie Review Log Book

TITLE:

GENRE: **YEAR:**

LENGTH: **DIRECTOR:**

DATE SEEN: **WHERE?**

COMPANY: **RATING (G, PG, G13, R):**

AWARDS:

ACTORS

MOVIE REVIEW (Storyline / Plot / Memorable Quotes)

RATINGS

CAST: **DRIECTOR:**

SCREENPLAY: **EFFECTS:**

COSTUMES: **MUSIC:**

PRODUCTION DESIGN: **CINEMATOGRAPHY:**

Overall Rating ★ ★ ★ ★ ★   *Watch Again?* **Y:** **/ N:**

Movie Review Log Book

TITLE:

GENRE: YEAR:

LENGTH: DIRECTOR:

DATE SEEN: WHERE?

COMPANY: RATING (G, PG, G13, R):

AWARDS:

ACTORS

MOVIE REVIEW (Storyline / Plot / Memorable Quotes)

RATINGS

CAST: DRIECTOR:

SCREENPLAY: EFFECTS:

COSTUMES: MUSIC:

PRODUCTION DESIGN: CINEMATOGRAPHY:

Overall Rating ★ ★ ★ ★ ★   Watch Again? Y: / N:

Movie Review Log Book

TITLE:

GENRE: **YEAR:**

LENGTH: **DIRECTOR:**

DATE SEEN: **WHERE?**

COMPANY: **RATING (G, PG, G13, R):**

AWARDS:

ACTORS

....
....
....
....
....

MOVIE REVIEW (Storyline / Plot / Memorable Quotes)

....
....
....
....
....
....
....
....
....
....
....
....

RATINGS

CAST: **DRIECTOR:**

SCREENPLAY: **EFFECTS:**

COSTUMES: **MUSIC:**

PRODUCTION DESIGN: **CINEMATOGRAPHY:**

Overall Rating ★ ★ ★ ★ ★ *Watch Again?* **Y:** **/ N:**

Movie Review Log Book

TITLE:

GENRE: **YEAR:**

LENGTH: **DIRECTOR:**

DATE SEEN: **WHERE?**

COMPANY: **RATING (G, PG, G13, R):**

AWARDS:

ACTORS

MOVIE REVIEW (Storyline / Plot / Memorable Quotes)

RATINGS	
CAST:	**DRIECTOR:**
SCREENPLAY:	**EFFECTS:**
COSTUMES:	**MUSIC:**
PRODUCTION DESIGN:	**CINEMATOGRAPHY:**

Overall Rating ★ ★ ★ ★ ★   *Watch Again?* **Y:**   **/ N:**

Movie Review Log Book

TITLE:

GENRE: **YEAR:**

LENGTH: **DIRECTOR:**

DATE SEEN: **WHERE?**

COMPANY: **RATING (G, PG, G13, R):**

AWARDS:

ACTORS

MOVIE REVIEW (Storyline / Plot / Memorable Quotes)

RATINGS

CAST:	DRIECTOR:
SCREENPLAY:	EFFECTS:
COSTUMES:	MUSIC:
PRODUCTION DESIGN:	CINEMATOGRAPHY:

Overall Rating ★ ★ ★ ★ ★   **Watch Again?** Y: / N:

Movie Review Log Book

TITLE:

GENRE: YEAR:

LENGTH: DIRECTOR:

DATE SEEN: WHERE?

COMPANY: RATING (G, PG, G13, R):

AWARDS:

ACTORS

....
....
....
....
....

MOVIE REVIEW (Storyline / Plot / Memorable Quotes)

....
....
....
....
....
....
....
....
....
....
....
....

RATINGS

CAST: DRIECTOR:

SCREENPLAY: EFFECTS:

COSTUMES: MUSIC:

PRODUCTION DESIGN: CINEMATOGRAPHY:

Overall Rating ★ ★ ★ ★ ★   Watch Again? Y: / N:

Movie Review Log Book

TITLE:

GENRE: **YEAR:**

LENGTH: **DIRECTOR:**

DATE SEEN: **WHERE?**

COMPANY: **RATING (G, PG, G13, R):**

AWARDS:

ACTORS

....
....
....
....
....

MOVIE REVIEW (Storyline / Plot / Memorable Quotes)

....
....
....
....
....
....
....
....
....
....
....

RATINGS

CAST:	**DRIECTOR:**
SCREENPLAY:	**EFFECTS:**
COSTUMES:	**MUSIC:**
PRODUCTION DESIGN:	**CINEMATOGRAPHY:**

Overall Rating ★ ★ ★ ★ ★ *Watch Again?* **Y:** / **N:**

Movie Review Log Book

TITLE:

GENRE: **YEAR:**

LENGTH: **DIRECTOR:**

DATE SEEN: **WHERE?**

COMPANY: **RATING (G, PG, G13, R):**

AWARDS:

ACTORS
....
....
....
....
....

MOVIE REVIEW (Storyline / Plot / Memorable Quotes)
....
....
....
....
....
....
....
....
....
....
....
....

RATINGS	
CAST:	**DRIECTOR:**
SCREENPLAY:	**EFFECTS:**
COSTUMES:	**MUSIC:**
PRODUCTION DESIGN:	**CINEMATOGRAPHY:**

Overall Rating ★ ★ ★ ★ ★ *Watch Again?* **Y:** **/ N:**

Movie Review Log Book

TITLE:

GENRE: **YEAR:**

LENGTH: **DIRECTOR:**

DATE SEEN: **WHERE?**

COMPANY: **RATING (G, PG, G13, R):**

AWARDS:

ACTORS

....
....
....
....
....

MOVIE REVIEW (Storyline / Plot / Memorable Quotes)

....
....
....
....
....
....
....
....
....
....
....
....

RATINGS

CAST: **DRIECTOR:**

SCREENPLAY: **EFFECTS:**

COSTUMES: **MUSIC:**

PRODUCTION DESIGN: **CINEMATOGRAPHY:**

Overall Rating ★ ★ ★ ★ ★   *Watch Again?* **Y: / N:**

Movie Review Log Book

TITLE:

GENRE: **YEAR:**

LENGTH: **DIRECTOR:**

DATE SEEN: **WHERE?**

COMPANY: **RATING (G, PG, G13, R):**

AWARDS:

ACTORS

....
....
....
....
....

MOVIE REVIEW (Storyline / Plot / Memorable Quotes)

....
....
....
....
....
....
....
....
....
....
....
....
....

RATINGS

CAST: **DRIECTOR:**

SCREENPLAY: **EFFECTS:**

COSTUMES: **MUSIC:**

PRODUCTION DESIGN: **CINEMATOGRAPHY:**

Overall Rating ★ ★ ★ ★ ★   *Watch Again?* **Y:**   **/ N:**

Movie Review Log Book

TITLE:

GENRE: **YEAR:**

LENGTH: **DIRECTOR:**

DATE SEEN: **WHERE?**

COMPANY: **RATING (G, PG, G13, R):**

AWARDS:

ACTORS

....
....
....
....
....

MOVIE REVIEW (Storyline / Plot / Memorable Quotes)

....
....
....
....
....
....
....
....
....
....
....
....

RATINGS

CAST: **DRIECTOR:**

SCREENPLAY: **EFFECTS:**

COSTUMES: **MUSIC:**

PRODUCTION DESIGN: **CINEMATOGRAPHY:**

Overall Rating ★ ★ ★ ★ ★   *Watch Again?* **Y: / N:**

Movie Review Log Book

TITLE:

GENRE: **YEAR:**

LENGTH: **DIRECTOR:**

DATE SEEN: **WHERE?**

COMPANY: **RATING (G, PG, G13, R):**

AWARDS:

ACTORS

MOVIE REVIEW (Storyline / Plot / Memorable Quotes)

RATINGS

CAST: **DRIECTOR:**

SCREENPLAY: **EFFECTS:**

COSTUMES: **MUSIC:**

PRODUCTION DESIGN: **CINEMATOGRAPHY:**

Overall Rating ★ ★ ★ ★ ★ *Watch Again?* **Y:** **/ N:**

Movie Review Log Book

TITLE:

GENRE: **YEAR:**

LENGTH: **DIRECTOR:**

DATE SEEN: **WHERE?**

COMPANY: **RATING (G, PG, G13, R):**

AWARDS:

ACTORS

MOVIE REVIEW (Storyline / Plot / Memorable Quotes)

RATINGS

CAST: **DRIECTOR:**

SCREENPLAY: **EFFECTS:**

COSTUMES: **MUSIC:**

PRODUCTION DESIGN: **CINEMATOGRAPHY:**

Overall Rating ★ ★ ★ ★ ★ *Watch Again?* **Y:** **/ N:**

Movie Review Log Book

TITLE:

GENRE: YEAR:

LENGTH: DIRECTOR:

DATE SEEN: WHERE?

COMPANY: RATING (G, PG, G13, R):

AWARDS:

ACTORS

....
....
....
....

MOVIE REVIEW (Storyline / Plot / Memorable Quotes)

....
....
....
....
....
....
....
....
....
....
....

RATINGS

CAST: DRIECTOR:

SCREENPLAY: EFFECTS:

COSTUMES: MUSIC:

PRODUCTION DESIGN: CINEMATOGRAPHY:

Overall Rating ★ ★ ★ ★ ★   *Watch Again?* Y: / N:

Movie Review Log Book

TITLE:

GENRE: **YEAR:**

LENGTH: **DIRECTOR:**

DATE SEEN: **WHERE?**

COMPANY: **RATING (G, PG, G13, R):**

AWARDS:

ACTORS

....
....
....
....
....

MOVIE REVIEW (Storyline / Plot / Memorable Quotes)

....
....
....
....
....
....
....
....
....
....
....
....
....

RATINGS

CAST: **DRIECTOR:**

SCREENPLAY: **EFFECTS:**

COSTUMES: **MUSIC:**

PRODUCTION DESIGN: **CINEMATOGRAPHY:**

Overall Rating ★ ★ ★ ★ ★   *Watch Again?* **Y:** **/ N:**

Movie Review Log Book

TITLE:

GENRE: **YEAR:**

LENGTH: **DIRECTOR:**

DATE SEEN: **WHERE?**

COMPANY: **RATING (G, PG, G13, R):**

AWARDS:

ACTORS

MOVIE REVIEW (Storyline / Plot / Memorable Quotes)

RATINGS

CAST: **DRIECTOR:**

SCREENPLAY: **EFFECTS:**

COSTUMES: **MUSIC:**

PRODUCTION DESIGN: **CINEMATOGRAPHY:**

Overall Rating ★ ★ ★ ★ ★   *Watch Again?* **Y:** **/ N:**

Movie Review Log Book

TITLE:

GENRE: **YEAR:**

LENGTH: **DIRECTOR:**

DATE SEEN: **WHERE?**

COMPANY: **RATING (G, PG, G13, R):**

AWARDS:

ACTORS

....
....
....
....
....

MOVIE REVIEW (Storyline / Plot / Memorable Quotes)

....
....
....
....
....
....
....
....
....
....
....
....

RATINGS

CAST: **DRIECTOR:**

SCREENPLAY: **EFFECTS:**

COSTUMES: **MUSIC:**

PRODUCTION DESIGN: **CINEMATOGRAPHY:**

Overall Rating ⭐ ⭐ ⭐ ⭐ ⭐   **Watch Again?** **Y:**   **/ N:**

Movie Review Log Book

TITLE:

GENRE: YEAR:

LENGTH: DIRECTOR:

DATE SEEN: WHERE?

COMPANY: RATING (G, PG, G13, R):

AWARDS:

ACTORS

....
....
....
....
....

MOVIE REVIEW (Storyline / Plot / Memorable Quotes)

....
....
....
....
....
....
....
....
....
....
....
....

RATINGS

CAST: DRIECTOR:

SCREENPLAY: EFFECTS:

COSTUMES: MUSIC:

PRODUCTION DESIGN: CINEMATOGRAPHY:

Overall Rating ★ ★ ★ ★ ★   Watch Again? Y: / N:

Movie Review Log Book

TITLE:

GENRE: **YEAR:**

LENGTH: **DIRECTOR:**

DATE SEEN: **WHERE?**

COMPANY: **RATING (G, PG, G13, R):**

AWARDS:

ACTORS

....
....
....
....
....

MOVIE REVIEW (Storyline / Plot / Memorable Quotes)

....
....
....
....
....
....
....
....
....
....
....

RATINGS

CAST: **DRIECTOR:**

SCREENPLAY: **EFFECTS:**

COSTUMES: **MUSIC:**

PRODUCTION DESIGN: **CINEMATOGRAPHY:**

Overall Rating ★ ★ ★ ★ ★   *Watch Again?* **Y:** **/ N:**

Movie Review Log Book

TITLE:

GENRE: **YEAR:**

LENGTH: **DIRECTOR:**

DATE SEEN: **WHERE?**

COMPANY: **RATING (G, PG, G13, R):**

AWARDS:

ACTORS

....
....
....
....
....

MOVIE REVIEW (Storyline / Plot / Memorable Quotes)

....
....
....
....
....
....
....
....
....
....
....

RATINGS

CAST: **DRIECTOR:**

SCREENPLAY: **EFFECTS:**

COSTUMES: **MUSIC:**

PRODUCTION DESIGN: **CINEMATOGRAPHY:**

Overall Rating ★ ★ ★ ★ ★   *Watch Again?* **Y:** / **N:**

Movie Review Log Book

TITLE:

GENRE: YEAR:

LENGTH: DIRECTOR:

DATE SEEN: WHERE?

COMPANY: RATING (G, PG, G13, R):

AWARDS:

ACTORS

....
....
....
....
....

MOVIE REVIEW (Storyline / Plot / Memorable Quotes)

....
....
....
....
....
....
....
....
....
....
....
....

RATINGS

CAST: DRIECTOR:

SCREENPLAY: EFFECTS:

COSTUMES: MUSIC:

PRODUCTION DESIGN: CINEMATOGRAPHY:

Overall Rating ★ ★ ★ ★ ★   Watch Again? Y: / N:

Movie Review Log Book

TITLE:

GENRE: **YEAR:**

LENGTH: **DIRECTOR:**

DATE SEEN: **WHERE?**

COMPANY: **RATING (G, PG, G13, R):**

AWARDS:

ACTORS

....
....
....
....
....

MOVIE REVIEW (Storyline / Plot / Memorable Quotes)

....
....
....
....
....
....
....
....
....
....
....
....

RATINGS

CAST: **DRIECTOR:**

SCREENPLAY: **EFFECTS:**

COSTUMES: **MUSIC:**

PRODUCTION DESIGN: **CINEMATOGRAPHY:**

Overall Rating ★ ★ ★ ★ ★   *Watch Again?* **Y:** **/ N:**

Movie Review Log Book

TITLE:

GENRE: **YEAR:**

LENGTH: **DIRECTOR:**

DATE SEEN: **WHERE?**

COMPANY: **RATING (G, PG, G13, R):**

AWARDS:

ACTORS

....
....
....
....
....

MOVIE REVIEW (Storyline / Plot / Memorable Quotes)

....
....
....
....
....
....
....
....
....
....
....

RATINGS

CAST: **DRIECTOR:**

SCREENPLAY: **EFFECTS:**

COSTUMES: **MUSIC:**

PRODUCTION DESIGN: **CINEMATOGRAPHY:**

Overall Rating ★ ★ ★ ★ ★   *Watch Again?* **Y:** **/ N:**

Movie Review Log Book

TITLE:

GENRE: **YEAR:**

LENGTH: **DIRECTOR:**

DATE SEEN: **WHERE?**

COMPANY: **RATING (G, PG, G13, R):**

AWARDS:

ACTORS
....
....
....
....
....

MOVIE REVIEW (Storyline / Plot / Memorable Quotes)
....
....
....
....
....
....
....
....
....
....
....
....

RATINGS	
CAST:	**DRIECTOR:**
SCREENPLAY:	**EFFECTS:**
COSTUMES:	**MUSIC:**
PRODUCTION DESIGN:	**CINEMATOGRAPHY:**

Overall Rating ★ ★ ★ ★ ★   *Watch Again?* **Y:**   **/ N:**

Movie Review Log Book

TITLE:

GENRE: **YEAR:**

LENGTH: **DIRECTOR:**

DATE SEEN: **WHERE?**

COMPANY: **RATING (G, PG, G13, R):**

AWARDS:

ACTORS

MOVIE REVIEW (Storyline / Plot / Memorable Quotes)

RATINGS

CAST:	**DRIECTOR:**
SCREENPLAY:	**EFFECTS:**
COSTUMES:	**MUSIC:**
PRODUCTION DESIGN:	**CINEMATOGRAPHY:**

Overall Rating ★ ★ ★ ★ ★   **Watch Again?** Y: / N:

Movie Review Log Book

TITLE:

GENRE: **YEAR:**

LENGTH: **DIRECTOR:**

DATE SEEN: **WHERE?**

COMPANY: **RATING (G, PG, G13, R):**

AWARDS:

ACTORS

....
....
....
....
....

MOVIE REVIEW (Storyline / Plot / Memorable Quotes)

....
....
....
....
....
....
....
....
....
....
....
....
....

RATINGS

CAST: **DRIECTOR:**

SCREENPLAY: **EFFECTS:**

COSTUMES: **MUSIC:**

PRODUCTION DESIGN: **CINEMATOGRAPHY:**

Overall Rating ★ ★ ★ ★ ★ *Watch Again?* **Y:** **/ N:**

Movie Review Log Book

TITLE:

GENRE: **YEAR:**

LENGTH: **DIRECTOR:**

DATE SEEN: **WHERE?**

COMPANY: **RATING (G, PG, G13, R):**

AWARDS:

ACTORS

....
....
....
....
....

MOVIE REVIEW (Storyline / Plot / Memorable Quotes)

....
....
....
....
....
....
....
....
....
....
....
....

RATINGS

CAST: **DRIECTOR:**

SCREENPLAY: **EFFECTS:**

COSTUMES: **MUSIC:**

PRODUCTION DESIGN: **CINEMATOGRAPHY:**

Overall Rating ★ ★ ★ ★ ★   *Watch Again?* **Y:** / **N:**

Movie Review Log Book

TITLE:

GENRE: **YEAR:**

LENGTH: **DIRECTOR:**

DATE SEEN: **WHERE?**

COMPANY: **RATING (G, PG, G13, R):**

AWARDS:

ACTORS

MOVIE REVIEW (Storyline / Plot / Memorable Quotes)

RATINGS

CAST: **DRIECTOR:**

SCREENPLAY: **EFFECTS:**

COSTUMES: **MUSIC:**

PRODUCTION DESIGN: **CINEMATOGRAPHY:**

Overall Rating ★ ★ ★ ★ ★ *Watch Again?* **Y:** **/ N:**

Movie Review Log Book

TITLE:

GENRE: **YEAR:**

LENGTH: **DIRECTOR:**

DATE SEEN: **WHERE?**

COMPANY: **RATING (G, PG, G13, R):**

AWARDS:

ACTORS

....
....
....
....
....

MOVIE REVIEW (Storyline / Plot / Memorable Quotes)

....
....
....
....
....
....
....
....
....
....
....
....

RATINGS

CAST: **DRIECTOR:**

SCREENPLAY: **EFFECTS:**

COSTUMES: **MUSIC:**

PRODUCTION DESIGN: **CINEMATOGRAPHY:**

Overall Rating ★ ★ ★ ★ ★   Watch Again? **Y:** **/ N:**

Movie Review Log Book

TITLE:

GENRE: **YEAR:**

LENGTH: **DIRECTOR:**

DATE SEEN: **WHERE?**

COMPANY: **RATING (G, PG, G13, R):**

AWARDS:

ACTORS

....
....
....
....
....

MOVIE REVIEW (Storyline / Plot / Memorable Quotes)

....
....
....
....
....
....
....
....
....
....
....
....

RATINGS

CAST: **DRIECTOR:**

SCREENPLAY: **EFFECTS:**

COSTUMES: **MUSIC:**

PRODUCTION DESIGN: **CINEMATOGRAPHY:**

Overall Rating ★ ★ ★ ★ ★   *Watch Again?* **Y:**   **/ N:**

Movie Review Log Book

TITLE:

GENRE: **YEAR:**

LENGTH: **DIRECTOR:**

DATE SEEN: **WHERE?**

COMPANY: **RATING (G, PG, G13, R):**

AWARDS:

ACTORS

MOVIE REVIEW (Storyline / Plot / Memorable Quotes)

RATINGS

CAST: **DRIECTOR:**

SCREENPLAY: **EFFECTS:**

COSTUMES: **MUSIC:**

PRODUCTION DESIGN: **CINEMATOGRAPHY:**

Overall Rating ★ ★ ★ ★ ★ *Watch Again?* **Y:** **/ N:**

Movie Review Log Book

TITLE:

GENRE: **YEAR:**

LENGTH: **DIRECTOR:**

DATE SEEN: **WHERE?**

COMPANY: **RATING (G, PG, G13, R):**

AWARDS:

ACTORS

....
....
....
....
....

MOVIE REVIEW (Storyline / Plot / Memorable Quotes)

....
....
....
....
....
....
....
....
....
....
....
....
....

RATINGS

CAST: **DRIECTOR:**

SCREENPLAY: **EFFECTS:**

COSTUMES: **MUSIC:**

PRODUCTION DESIGN: **CINEMATOGRAPHY:**

Overall Rating ★ ★ ★ ★ ★   *Watch Again?* **Y:** **/ N:**

Movie Review Log Book

TITLE:

GENRE: **YEAR:**

LENGTH: **DIRECTOR:**

DATE SEEN: **WHERE?**

COMPANY: **RATING (G, PG, G13, R):**

AWARDS:

ACTORS

MOVIE REVIEW (Storyline / Plot / Memorable Quotes)

RATINGS

CAST: **DRIECTOR:**

SCREENPLAY: **EFFECTS:**

COSTUMES: **MUSIC:**

PRODUCTION DESIGN: **CINEMATOGRAPHY:**

Overall Rating ★ ★ ★ ★ ★ *Watch Again?* **Y:** **/ N:**

Movie Review Log Book

TITLE:

GENRE: **YEAR:**

LENGTH: **DIRECTOR:**

DATE SEEN: **WHERE?**

COMPANY: **RATING (G, PG, G13, R):**

AWARDS:

ACTORS

MOVIE REVIEW (Storyline / Plot / Memorable Quotes)

RATINGS	
CAST:	**DRIECTOR:**
SCREENPLAY:	**EFFECTS:**
COSTUMES:	**MUSIC:**
PRODUCTION DESIGN:	**CINEMATOGRAPHY:**

Overall Rating ★ ★ ★ ★ ★   *Watch Again?* **Y:** **/ N:**

Movie Review Log Book

TITLE:

GENRE: **YEAR:**

LENGTH: **DIRECTOR:**

DATE SEEN: **WHERE?**

COMPANY: **RATING (G, PG, G13, R):**

AWARDS:

ACTORS

....
....
....
....
....

MOVIE REVIEW (Storyline / Plot / Memorable Quotes)

....
....
....
....
....
....
....
....
....
....
....

RATINGS

CAST: **DRIECTOR:**

SCREENPLAY: **EFFECTS:**

COSTUMES: **MUSIC:**

PRODUCTION DESIGN: **CINEMATOGRAPHY:**

Overall Rating ★ ★ ★ ★ ★ *Watch Again?* **Y:** **/ N:**

Movie Review Log Book

TITLE:

GENRE: **YEAR:**

LENGTH: **DIRECTOR:**

DATE SEEN: **WHERE?**

COMPANY: **RATING (G, PG, G13, R):**

AWARDS:

ACTORS

....
....
....
....
....

MOVIE REVIEW (Storyline / Plot / Memorable Quotes)

....
....
....
....
....
....
....
....
....
....
....
....

RATINGS

CAST:	DRIECTOR:
SCREENPLAY:	EFFECTS:
COSTUMES:	MUSIC:
PRODUCTION DESIGN:	CINEMATOGRAPHY:

Overall Rating ★ ★ ★ ★ ★   **Watch Again?** Y: / N:

Movie Review Log Book

TITLE:

GENRE: | **YEAR:**

LENGTH: | **DIRECTOR:**

DATE SEEN: | **WHERE?**

COMPANY: | **RATING (G, PG, G13, R):**

AWARDS:

ACTORS

....
....
....
....
....

MOVIE REVIEW (Storyline / Plot / Memorable Quotes)

....
....
....
....
....
....
....
....
....
....
....
....
....

RATINGS

CAST: | **DRIECTOR:**

SCREENPLAY: | **EFFECTS:**

COSTUMES: | **MUSIC:**

PRODUCTION DESIGN: | **CINEMATOGRAPHY:**

Overall Rating ★ ★ ★ ★ ★   *Watch Again?* **Y:** / **N:**

Movie Review Log Book

TITLE:

GENRE: **YEAR:**

LENGTH: **DIRECTOR:**

DATE SEEN: **WHERE?**

COMPANY: **RATING (G, PG, G13, R):**

AWARDS:

ACTORS

MOVIE REVIEW (Storyline / Plot / Memorable Quotes)

RATINGS

CAST: **DRIECTOR:**

SCREENPLAY: **EFFECTS:**

COSTUMES: **MUSIC:**

PRODUCTION DESIGN: **CINEMATOGRAPHY:**

Overall Rating ★ ★ ★ ★ ★ *Watch Again?* **Y:** **/ N:**

Movie Review Log Book

TITLE:

GENRE: **YEAR:**

LENGTH: **DIRECTOR:**

DATE SEEN: **WHERE?**

COMPANY: **RATING (G, PG, G13, R):**

AWARDS:

ACTORS

....
....
....
....
....

MOVIE REVIEW (Storyline / Plot / Memorable Quotes)

....
....
....
....
....
....
....
....
....
....
....
....

RATINGS

CAST: **DRIECTOR:**

SCREENPLAY: **EFFECTS:**

COSTUMES: **MUSIC:**

PRODUCTION DESIGN: **CINEMATOGRAPHY:**

Overall Rating ★ ★ ★ ★ ★   *Watch Again?* **Y:** **/ N:**

Movie Review Log Book

TITLE:

GENRE: **YEAR:**

LENGTH: **DIRECTOR:**

DATE SEEN: **WHERE?**

COMPANY: **RATING (G, PG, G13, R):**

AWARDS:

ACTORS

....
....
....
....
....

MOVIE REVIEW (Storyline / Plot / Memorable Quotes)

....
....
....
....
....
....
....
....
....
....
....
....
....

RATINGS

CAST: **DRIECTOR:**

SCREENPLAY: **EFFECTS:**

COSTUMES: **MUSIC:**

PRODUCTION DESIGN: **CINEMATOGRAPHY:**

Overall Rating ★ ★ ★ ★ ★   *Watch Again?* **Y:** **/ N:**

Movie Review Log Book

TITLE:

GENRE: **YEAR:**

LENGTH: **DIRECTOR:**

DATE SEEN: **WHERE?**

COMPANY: **RATING (G, PG, G13, R):**

AWARDS:

ACTORS

....
....
....
....
....

MOVIE REVIEW (Storyline / Plot / Memorable Quotes)

....
....
....
....
....
....
....
....
....
....
....
....
....

RATINGS

CAST: **DRIECTOR:**

SCREENPLAY: **EFFECTS:**

COSTUMES: **MUSIC:**

PRODUCTION DESIGN: **CINEMATOGRAPHY:**

Overall Rating ★ ★ ★ ★ ★   *Watch Again?* **Y:** **/ N:**

Movie Review Log Book

TITLE:

GENRE: **YEAR:**

LENGTH: **DIRECTOR:**

DATE SEEN: **WHERE?**

COMPANY: **RATING (G, PG, G13, R):**

AWARDS:

ACTORS

MOVIE REVIEW (Storyline / Plot / Memorable Quotes)

RATINGS

CAST: **DRIECTOR:**

SCREENPLAY: **EFFECTS:**

COSTUMES: **MUSIC:**

PRODUCTION DESIGN: **CINEMATOGRAPHY:**

Overall Rating ⭐ ⭐ ⭐ ⭐ ⭐   *Watch Again?* **Y:** **/ N:**

Movie Review Log Book

TITLE:

GENRE: **YEAR:**

LENGTH: **DIRECTOR:**

DATE SEEN: **WHERE?**

COMPANY: **RATING (G, PG, G13, R):**

AWARDS:

ACTORS

MOVIE REVIEW (Storyline / Plot / Memorable Quotes)

RATINGS

CAST: **DRIECTOR:**

SCREENPLAY: **EFFECTS:**

COSTUMES: **MUSIC:**

PRODUCTION DESIGN: **CINEMATOGRAPHY:**

Overall Rating ★ ★ ★ ★ ★ *Watch Again?* **Y: / N:**

Movie Review Log Book

TITLE:

GENRE: **YEAR:**

LENGTH: **DIRECTOR:**

DATE SEEN: **WHERE?**

COMPANY: **RATING (G, PG, G13, R):**

AWARDS:

ACTORS

MOVIE REVIEW (Storyline / Plot / Memorable Quotes)

RATINGS

CAST: **DRIECTOR:**

SCREENPLAY: **EFFECTS:**

COSTUMES: **MUSIC:**

PRODUCTION DESIGN: **CINEMATOGRAPHY:**

Overall Rating ★ ★ ★ ★ ★   *Watch Again?* **Y:** **/ N:**

Movie Review Log Book

TITLE:

GENRE: **YEAR:**

LENGTH: **DIRECTOR:**

DATE SEEN: **WHERE?**

COMPANY: **RATING (G, PG, G13, R):**

AWARDS:

ACTORS

....
....
....
....
....

MOVIE REVIEW (Storyline / Plot / Memorable Quotes)

....
....
....
....
....
....
....
....
....
....
....

RATINGS

CAST: **DRIECTOR:**

SCREENPLAY: **EFFECTS:**

COSTUMES: **MUSIC:**

PRODUCTION DESIGN: **CINEMATOGRAPHY:**

Overall Rating ⭐ ⭐ ⭐ ⭐ ⭐   *Watch Again?* **Y:**   **/ N:**

Movie Review Log Book

TITLE:

GENRE: **YEAR:**

LENGTH: **DIRECTOR:**

DATE SEEN: **WHERE?**

COMPANY: **RATING (G, PG, G13, R):**

AWARDS:

ACTORS

....
....
....
....
....

MOVIE REVIEW (Storyline / Plot / Memorable Quotes)

....
....
....
....
....
....
....
....
....
....
....
....

RATINGS

CAST: **DRIECTOR:**

SCREENPLAY: **EFFECTS:**

COSTUMES: **MUSIC:**

PRODUCTION DESIGN: **CINEMATOGRAPHY:**

Overall Rating ★ ★ ★ ★ ★ *Watch Again?* **Y:** **/ N:**

Movie Review Log Book

TITLE:

GENRE: **YEAR:**

LENGTH: **DIRECTOR:**

DATE SEEN: **WHERE?**

COMPANY: **RATING (G, PG, G13, R):**

AWARDS:

ACTORS

MOVIE REVIEW (Storyline / Plot / Memorable Quotes)

RATINGS

CAST: **DRIECTOR:**

SCREENPLAY: **EFFECTS:**

COSTUMES: **MUSIC:**

PRODUCTION DESIGN: **CINEMATOGRAPHY:**

Overall Rating ★ ★ ★ ★ ★   *Watch Again?* **Y:** **/ N:**

Movie Review Log Book

TITLE:

GENRE: **YEAR:**

LENGTH: **DIRECTOR:**

DATE SEEN: **WHERE?**

COMPANY: **RATING (G, PG, G13, R):**

AWARDS:

ACTORS

....
....
....
....
....

MOVIE REVIEW (Storyline / Plot / Memorable Quotes)

....
....
....
....
....
....
....
....
....
....
....
....

RATINGS

CAST: **DRIECTOR:**

SCREENPLAY: **EFFECTS:**

COSTUMES: **MUSIC:**

PRODUCTION DESIGN: **CINEMATOGRAPHY:**

Overall Rating ★ ★ ★ ★ ★ *Watch Again?* **Y:** **/ N:**

Movie Review Log Book

TITLE:

GENRE: **YEAR:**

LENGTH: **DIRECTOR:**

DATE SEEN: **WHERE?**

COMPANY: **RATING (G, PG, G13, R):**

AWARDS:

ACTORS

....
....
....
....
....

MOVIE REVIEW (Storyline / Plot / Memorable Quotes)

....
....
....
....
....
....
....
....
....
....
....
....
....

RATINGS

CAST: **DRIECTOR:**

SCREENPLAY: **EFFECTS:**

COSTUMES: **MUSIC:**

PRODUCTION DESIGN: **CINEMATOGRAPHY:**

Overall Rating ★ ★ ★ ★ ★   *Watch Again?* **Y:** / **N:**

Movie Review Log Book

TITLE:

GENRE: **YEAR:**

LENGTH: **DIRECTOR:**

DATE SEEN: **WHERE?**

COMPANY: **RATING (G, PG, G13, R):**

AWARDS:

ACTORS

....
....
....
....
....

MOVIE REVIEW (Storyline / Plot / Memorable Quotes)

....
....
....
....
....
....
....
....
....
....
....
....

RATINGS

CAST: **DRIECTOR:**

SCREENPLAY: **EFFECTS:**

COSTUMES: **MUSIC:**

PRODUCTION DESIGN: **CINEMATOGRAPHY:**

Overall Rating ★ ★ ★ ★ ★   *Watch Again?* **Y:** **/ N:**

Movie Review Log Book

TITLE:

GENRE: **YEAR:**

LENGTH: **DIRECTOR:**

DATE SEEN: **WHERE?**

COMPANY: **RATING (G, PG, G13, R):**

AWARDS:

ACTORS

MOVIE REVIEW (Storyline / Plot / Memorable Quotes)

RATINGS

CAST: **DRIECTOR:**

SCREENPLAY: **EFFECTS:**

COSTUMES: **MUSIC:**

PRODUCTION DESIGN: **CINEMATOGRAPHY:**

Overall Rating ★ ★ ★ ★ ★   *Watch Again?* **Y:** **/ N:**

Movie Review Log Book

TITLE:

GENRE: **YEAR:**

LENGTH: **DIRECTOR:**

DATE SEEN: **WHERE?**

COMPANY: **RATING (G, PG, G13, R):**

AWARDS:

ACTORS

....
....
....
....
....

MOVIE REVIEW (Storyline / Plot / Memorable Quotes)

....
....
....
....
....
....
....
....
....
....

RATINGS

CAST: **DRIECTOR:**

SCREENPLAY: **EFFECTS:**

COSTUMES: **MUSIC:**

PRODUCTION DESIGN: **CINEMATOGRAPHY:**

Overall Rating ★ ★ ★ ★ ★ *Watch Again?* **Y:** **/ N:**

Movie Review Log Book

TITLE:

GENRE: **YEAR:**

LENGTH: **DIRECTOR:**

DATE SEEN: **WHERE?**

COMPANY: **RATING (G, PG, G13, R):**

AWARDS:

ACTORS

....
....
....
....
....

MOVIE REVIEW (Storyline / Plot / Memorable Quotes)

....
....
....
....
....
....
....
....
....
....
....

RATINGS

CAST: **DRIECTOR:**

SCREENPLAY: **EFFECTS:**

COSTUMES: **MUSIC:**

PRODUCTION DESIGN: **CINEMATOGRAPHY:**

Overall Rating ★ ★ ★ ★ ★   *Watch Again?* **Y:** **/ N:**

Movie Review Log Book

TITLE:

GENRE: **YEAR:**

LENGTH: **DIRECTOR:**

DATE SEEN: **WHERE?**

COMPANY: **RATING (G, PG, G13, R):**

AWARDS:

ACTORS

....
....
....
....

MOVIE REVIEW (Storyline / Plot / Memorable Quotes)

....
....
....
....
....
....
....
....
....
....
....

RATINGS

CAST: **DRIECTOR:**

SCREENPLAY: **EFFECTS:**

COSTUMES: **MUSIC:**

PRODUCTION DESIGN: **CINEMATOGRAPHY:**

Overall Rating ⭐ ⭐ ⭐ ⭐ ⭐   *Watch Again?* **Y: / N:**

Movie Review Log Book

TITLE:

GENRE: **YEAR:**

LENGTH: **DIRECTOR:**

DATE SEEN: **WHERE?**

COMPANY: **RATING (G, PG, G13, R):**

AWARDS:

ACTORS

....
....
....
....
....

MOVIE REVIEW (Storyline / Plot / Memorable Quotes)

....
....
....
....
....
....
....
....
....
....
....
....

RATINGS

CAST: **DRIECTOR:**

SCREENPLAY: **EFFECTS:**

COSTUMES: **MUSIC:**

PRODUCTION DESIGN: **CINEMATOGRAPHY:**

Overall Rating ★ ★ ★ ★ ★   **Watch Again?** Y: / N:

Movie Review Log Book

TITLE:

GENRE: **YEAR:**

LENGTH: **DIRECTOR:**

DATE SEEN: **WHERE?**

COMPANY: **RATING (G, PG, G13, R):**

AWARDS:

ACTORS

MOVIE REVIEW (Storyline / Plot / Memorable Quotes)

RATINGS

CAST: **DRIECTOR:**

SCREENPLAY: **EFFECTS:**

COSTUMES: **MUSIC:**

PRODUCTION DESIGN: **CINEMATOGRAPHY:**

Overall Rating ★ ★ ★ ★ ★ *Watch Again?* **Y:** **/ N:**

Movie Review Log Book

TITLE:

GENRE: **YEAR:**

LENGTH: **DIRECTOR:**

DATE SEEN: **WHERE?**

COMPANY: **RATING (G, PG, G13, R):**

AWARDS:

ACTORS

....
....
....
....
....

MOVIE REVIEW (Storyline / Plot / Memorable Quotes)

....
....
....
....
....
....
....
....
....
....
....
....

RATINGS

CAST: **DRIECTOR:**

SCREENPLAY: **EFFECTS:**

COSTUMES: **MUSIC:**

PRODUCTION DESIGN: **CINEMATOGRAPHY:**

Overall Rating ★ ★ ★ ★ ★   *Watch Again?* **Y:** **/ N:**

Movie Review Log Book

TITLE:

GENRE: **YEAR:**

LENGTH: **DIRECTOR:**

DATE SEEN: **WHERE?**

COMPANY: **RATING (G, PG, G13, R):**

AWARDS:

ACTORS

....
....
....
....
....

MOVIE REVIEW (Storyline / Plot / Memorable Quotes)

....
....
....
....
....
....
....
....
....
....
....
....
....

RATINGS

CAST: **DRIECTOR:**

SCREENPLAY: **EFFECTS:**

COSTUMES: **MUSIC:**

PRODUCTION DESIGN: **CINEMATOGRAPHY:**

Overall Rating ★ ★ ★ ★ ★   *Watch Again?* **Y:**   **/ N:**

Movie Review Log Book

TITLE:

GENRE: **YEAR:**

LENGTH: **DIRECTOR:**

DATE SEEN: **WHERE?**

COMPANY: **RATING (G, PG, G13, R):**

AWARDS:

ACTORS

MOVIE REVIEW (Storyline / Plot / Memorable Quotes)

RATINGS

CAST: **DRIECTOR:**

SCREENPLAY: **EFFECTS:**

COSTUMES: **MUSIC:**

PRODUCTION DESIGN: **CINEMATOGRAPHY:**

Overall Rating ★ ★ ★ ★ ★ *Watch Again?* **Y: / N:**

Movie Review Log Book

TITLE:

GENRE: **YEAR:**

LENGTH: **DIRECTOR:**

DATE SEEN: **WHERE?**

COMPANY: **RATING (G, PG, G13, R):**

AWARDS:

ACTORS

....
....
....
....
....

MOVIE REVIEW (Storyline / Plot / Memorable Quotes)

....
....
....
....
....
....
....
....
....
....
....

RATINGS

CAST: **DRIECTOR:**

SCREENPLAY: **EFFECTS:**

COSTUMES: **MUSIC:**

PRODUCTION DESIGN: **CINEMATOGRAPHY:**

Overall Rating ★ ★ ★ ★ ★   *Watch Again?* **Y:** **/ N:**

Movie Review Log Book

TITLE:

GENRE:　　　　　　　　　　　　　　　**YEAR:**

LENGTH:　　　　　　　**DIRECTOR:**

DATE SEEN:　　　　　　**WHERE?**

COMPANY:　　　　　　　　　　　**RATING (G, PG, G13, R):**

AWARDS:

ACTORS

....
....
....
....
....

MOVIE REVIEW (Storyline / Plot / Memorable Quotes)

....
....
....
....
....
....
....
....
....
....
....
....

RATINGS

CAST:　　　　　　　　　**DRIECTOR:**

SCREENPLAY:　　　　　　**EFFECTS:**

COSTUMES:　　　　　　　**MUSIC:**

PRODUCTION DESIGN:　　　**CINEMATOGRAPHY:**

Overall Rating ★ ★ ★ ★ ★　　*Watch Again?* **Y:** **/ N:**

Movie Review Log Book

TITLE:

GENRE: **YEAR:**

LENGTH: **DIRECTOR:**

DATE SEEN: **WHERE?**

COMPANY: **RATING (G, PG, G13, R):**

AWARDS:

ACTORS

MOVIE REVIEW (Storyline / Plot / Memorable Quotes)

RATINGS

CAST: **DRIECTOR:**

SCREENPLAY: **EFFECTS:**

COSTUMES: **MUSIC:**

PRODUCTION DESIGN: **CINEMATOGRAPHY:**

Overall Rating ★ ★ ★ ★ ★   *Watch Again?* **Y:** **/ N:**

Movie Review Log Book

TITLE:

GENRE: **YEAR:**

LENGTH: **DIRECTOR:**

DATE SEEN: **WHERE?**

COMPANY: **RATING (G, PG, G13, R):**

AWARDS:

ACTORS

MOVIE REVIEW (Storyline / Plot / Memorable Quotes)

RATINGS

CAST: **DRIECTOR:**

SCREENPLAY: **EFFECTS:**

COSTUMES: **MUSIC:**

PRODUCTION DESIGN: **CINEMATOGRAPHY:**

Overall Rating ★ ★ ★ ★ ★   *Watch Again?* **Y: / N:**

Movie Review Log Book

TITLE:

GENRE: **YEAR:**

LENGTH: **DIRECTOR:**

DATE SEEN: **WHERE?**

COMPANY: **RATING (G, PG, G13, R):**

AWARDS:

ACTORS

MOVIE REVIEW (Storyline / Plot / Memorable Quotes)

RATINGS

CAST: **DRIECTOR:**

SCREENPLAY: **EFFECTS:**

COSTUMES: **MUSIC:**

PRODUCTION DESIGN: **CINEMATOGRAPHY:**

Overall Rating ★ ★ ★ ★ ★   *Watch Again?* **Y:**   **/ N:**

MOVIE REVIEWS
—LOG BOOK—

Are you enjoying this awesome Log Book?

If so, please leave us a review. We are very interested in your feedback
to create even better products for you to enjoy shortly.

**Shopping for Log Books can be fun.
Visit our website at amazing-notebooks.com or scan the QR
code below to see all of our awesome and creative products!**

Thank you very much!

Amazing Notebooks

www.amazing-notebooks.com

Printed in Great Britain
by Amazon